Snow Patrol · A Hundred Mil

WISE PUBLICATIONS
part of The Music Sales Group
London / New York / Paris / Sydney / Copenhagen / Berlin / Madrid / Tokyo

Published by
Wise Publications
14-15 Berners Street, London W1T 3LJ, UK.

Exclusive distributors:
Music Sales Limited
Distribution Centre, Newmarket Road,
Bury St Edmunds, Suffolk, IP33 3YB, UK.

Music Sales Pty Limited
20 Resolution Drive, Caringbah, NSW 2229, Australia.

Order No. AM996039
ISBN 978-1-84772-847-0

Arranged by Derek Jones & Jack Long.
Music processed by Paul Ewers Music Design.
Edited by Fiona Bolton.

Printed in the EU.

If There's A Rocket Tie Me To It

Words & Music by Paul Wilson, Gary Lightbody,
Jonathan Quinn, Nathan Connolly & Tom Simpson

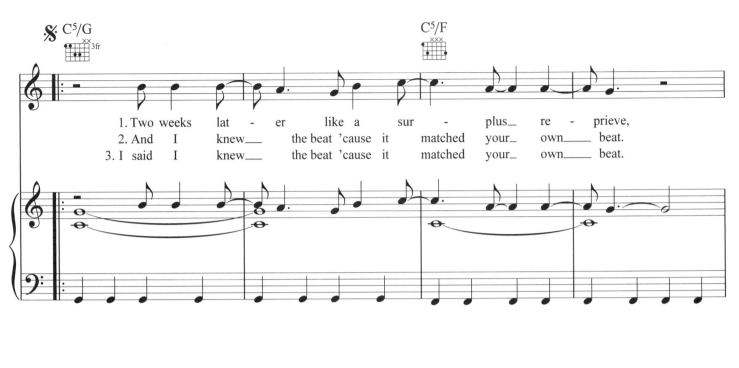

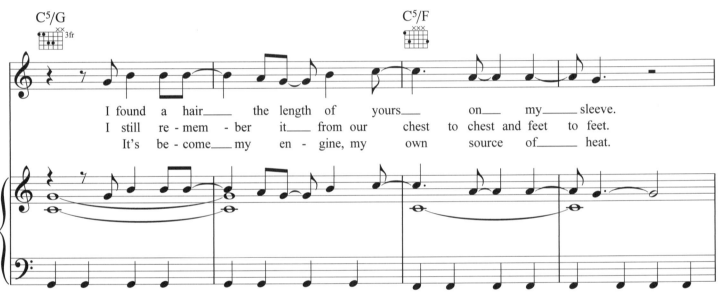

it turned to pur - ple and a pulse___ formed in - side.
of ov - ens, aer - o - planes and of dis - tant___ car___ horns.
Ev - 'ry hum and ech - o and crash___ paints my___ cave.

1.

A fire,___ a fire.___
I break, you don't.___

You can on - ly take___ what you___
I was al - ways set___ to self-

___ can car - ry.
- de - struct___ though.

A pulse,___ your pulse.___
The fire,___ the fire,___

It's the
it

CRACK THE SHUTTERS

Words & Music by Paul Wilson, Gary Lightbody,
Jonathan Quinn, Nathan Connolly & Tom Simpson

1. You cool your bed - warm hands ____ down ____ on the bro-
2. It's been min - utes, it's been days, it's been

- ken ____ ra - di - a - tor. ____
all I ____ will re - mem - ber. ____

11

I could sit for hours find-ing new ways to be awed each_ min - ute

'cause the day-light seems to want you just___ as much as I want you.___

To Coda ⊕

D.S. al Coda

Crack the

⊕ Coda

Take Back The City

Words & Music by Paul Wilson, Gary Lightbody,
Jonathan Quinn, Nathan Connolly & Tom Simpson

1. Take back the cit-y for your-self to-night. I'll take back the cit-y for me.
2. All these years la-ter and it's kill-ing me. Your bro-ken re-cords in words.
3. Tell me you nev-er want-ed more than this and I will stop talk-ing now.

18

LIFEBOATS

Words & Music by Paul Wilson, Gary Lightbody,
Jonathan Quinn, Nathan Connolly & Tom Simpson

1. Hold on, hold on, let me get the words out be-fore I burst.
2. Sing out, sing out, the si-lence on-ly eats us from the in-side up.

20

life is way too short to scream and shout.
you said it in a way that showed you really cared.

Flashed up in my wildest dreams, the dark red

blood streams, stretching out like vast cracked ice.

The veins of you, the veins of me, like great for-

-est trees, push-ing through___ and on and in. Glid-ing like a sat-

- el-lite in the bro-ken night. And when I wake___you're there, I'm saved.___

Your love is life___piled tight and high, set a-gainst the sky, that seems to ba-

-lance on its___ own.___

22

The Golden Floor

Words & Music by Paul Wilson, Gary Lightbody,
Jonathan Quinn, Nathan Connolly & Tom Simpson

1. Tell me that you want to dance.___ I want to feel your pulse on
(4.) fold - ed in the bread you made.___ You're cold un - til my bod - y

mine.___ Just treat me like a sto - len glance___ to your - self.
bathes___ you in the heat I kept a - side___ all these___ days.

To Coda ⊕

2. A dark shape on a gold - en floor,___ a sleep - ing
(3.) peas - ant in your prin - cess arms,___

plan - et with a molt - en core.___ From a - bove we'd cut a slow eight
pen - ni - less with on - ly charm. As we're lev - elled by the low, hot

shape___ and much___ more.___
lights___ and dis - armed.___

3. I'm a

25

I'm not a-fraid of an - y-thing,___ e - ven___ time.___

It -'ll eke a-way at ev -'ry- thing,___ but we'll be___ fine.

Vocal ad lib.

D.S. al Coda

4. I'm

Please Just Take These Photos From My Hands

Words & Music by Paul Wilson, Gary Lightbody,
Jonathan Quinn, Nathan Connolly & Tom Simpson

Original key D♭ major

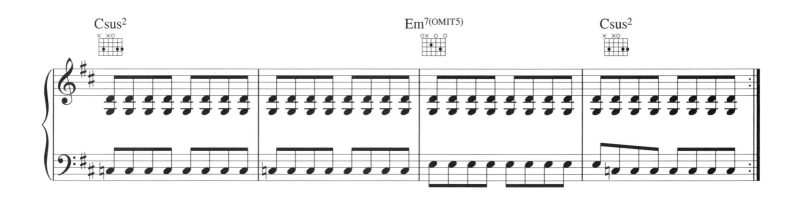

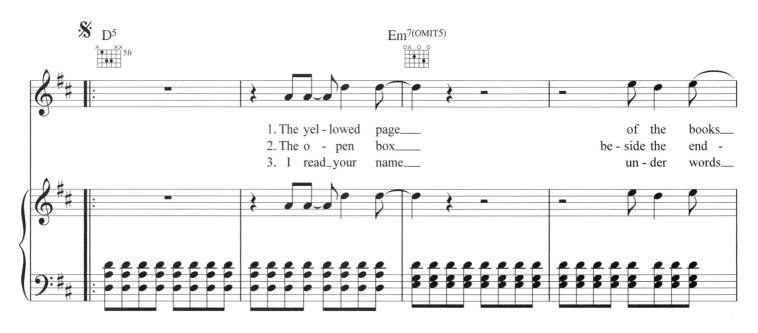

1. The yel-lowed page___ of the books___
2. The o-pen box___ be-side the end-
3. I read_your name___ un-der words__

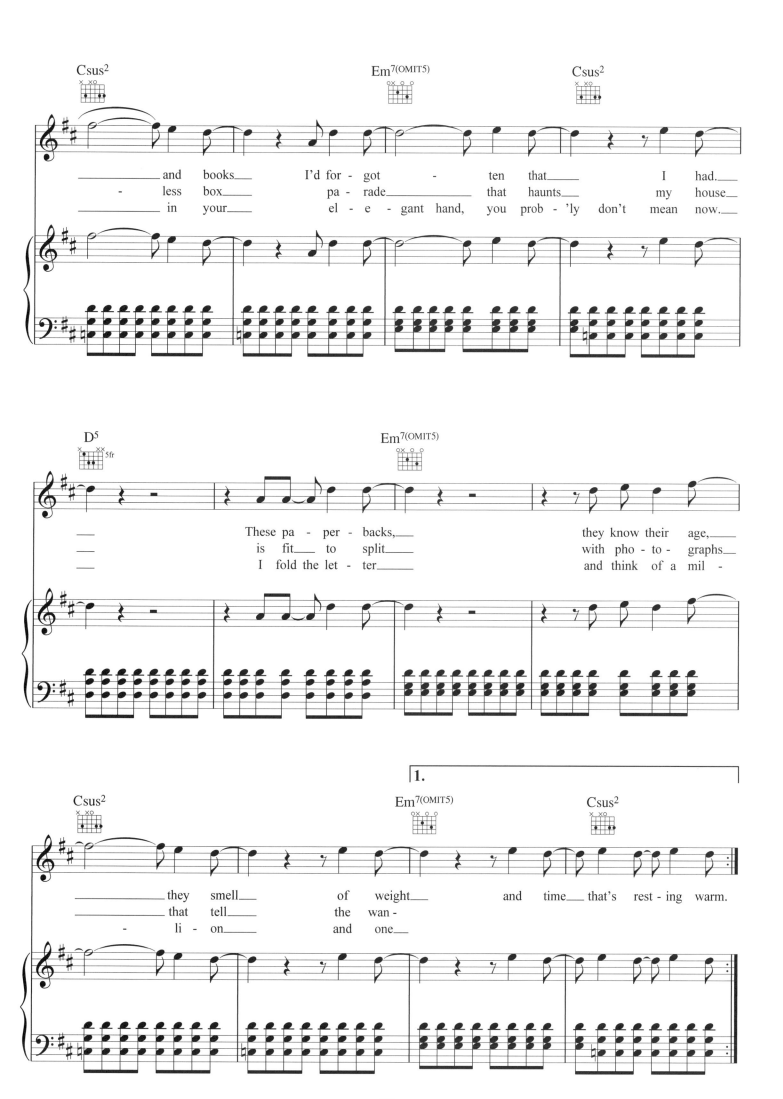

32

ENGINES

Words & Music by Paul Wilson, Gary Lightbody,
Jonathan Quinn, Nathan Connolly & Tom Simpson

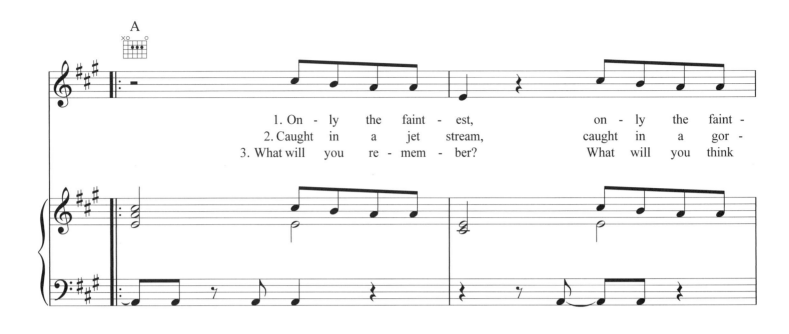

1. On - ly the faint - est,   on - ly the faint -
2. Caught in a jet stream,   caught in a gor -
3. What will you re - mem - ber? What will you think

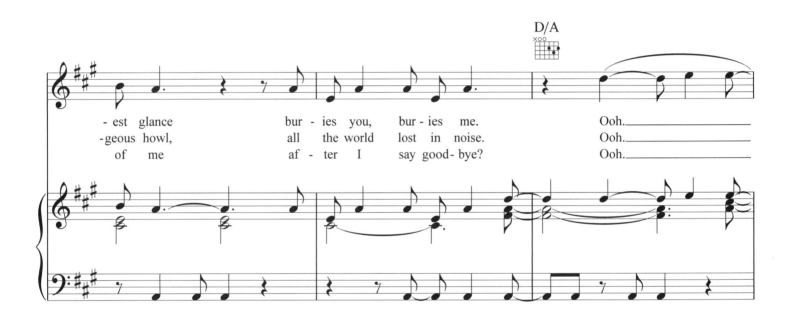

- est glance   bur - ies you,   bur - ies me.   Ooh._____
-geous howl,   all the world   lost in noise.   Ooh._____
of me   af - ter I   say good- bye?   Ooh._____

__   Ooh._____   Ooh._____
__   Ooh._____   Ooh._____
__   Ooh._____   Ooh._____

So fire your en - gine, see if I give a damn. We'll
Use me for - ev - er, use me as rock - et fuel. I'll
Re - turn - ing bod - ies, plants and the sand you'll squeeze in -

be dust in - stant - ly. Ooh._____ Ooh._____
be air, I'll be fire. Ooh._____ Ooh._____
- be - tween shoe - less feet. Ooh._____ Ooh._____

Ooh._____
Ooh._____
Ooh._____

I know you love me like the end - less roar of

mod - ern life.___ I know you love me like the laugh -

- ter and the kissed back tears.___

I know you love me like the past,___ the now, the com - ing years.___

Set Down Your Glass

Words & Music by Paul Wilson, Gary Lightbody,
Jonathan Quinn, Nathan Connolly & Tom Simpson

1. Just close your eyes and count to five.
2. Set down your glass, I paint-ed this

Let's craft the on-ly thing we know in-to sur-prise.
to look like you and me for-ev-er as we're now.

The Planets Bend Between Us

Words & Music by Paul Wilson, Gary Lightbody,
Jonathan Quinn, Nathan Connolly & Tom Simpson

1.The win - ter's marked the earth. It's floored
(2.) - ing speech bub-bles seem to hold

46

Disaster Button

**Words & Music by Paul Wilson, Gary Lightbody,
Jonathan Quinn, Nathan Connolly & Tom Simpson**

2. Ripped-up tick-et stubs___ con-fet-tied on___ the floor.___
3. Cool your beans,___ my son.___ You look a mess.___
4. Hit that but-ton there.___ The one that just___ says wrong.___

___ It dawned on me___ I'd seen___ it all.___
___ No-one's get-ting out___ of here___
___ And we'll lose our minds to all___ our fav -

be-fore.___ - - 'rite songs.
to-night.___

Throw for-ward to lat - er. You look light___ on your feet.
And sud-den-ly___ it lifts the roof___ off the place.

51

The Lightning Strike

(i) What If This Storm Ends?

Words & Music by Paul Wilson, Gary Lightbody,
Jonathan Quinn, Nathan Connolly & Tom Simpson

1. What if___ this storm___ ends?   And I don't see___ you

as___ you are now   ev-er___ a-gain._

2. The per-fect ha-lo   of gold hair   and light-ning

sets___ you off a-gainst_   the plan-et's last___dance.

3. Just for___ a min-ute   the sil-ver-forked_ sky
(4.)___ us,   like I___ have found_ you,

lit___ you up like a star___ that I will fol - low.
I___ don't wan-na run;___ just o-ver - whelm___ me.

4. And now it's found

5. What if this storm___

boils.
- less.

1.

7. I want to   see

2.

What if____ this storm

The Lightning Strike

(ii) The Sunlight Through The Flags

Words & Music by Paul Wilson, Gary Lightbody,
Jonathan Quinn, Nathan Connolly & Tom Simpson

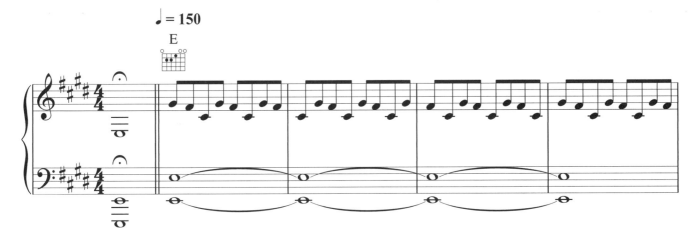

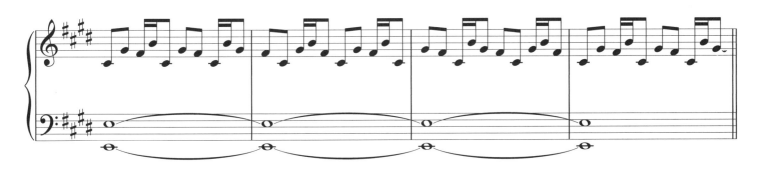

1. From here the car - a - vans are

hon - - ey jars.

1. These ac - ci -

Why don't you rest your frag - ile bones?

64

min - ute a - go you looked a - lone.

Stop wav - ing your arms, you're safe and

dry. Breathe in and drink up the

win - ter sky.

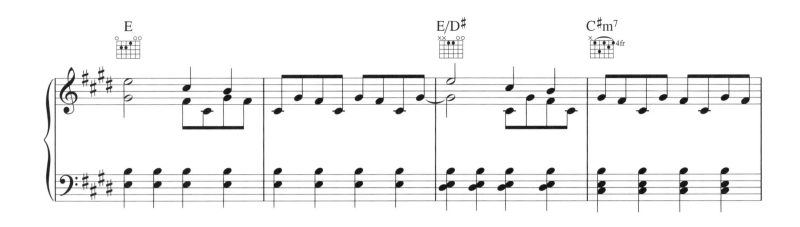

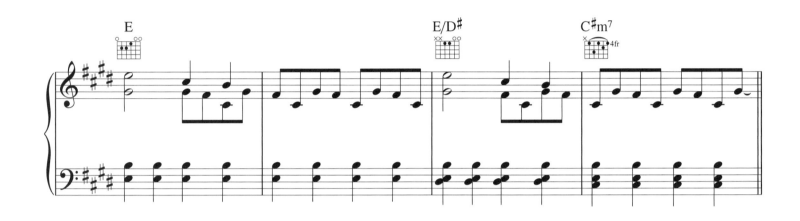

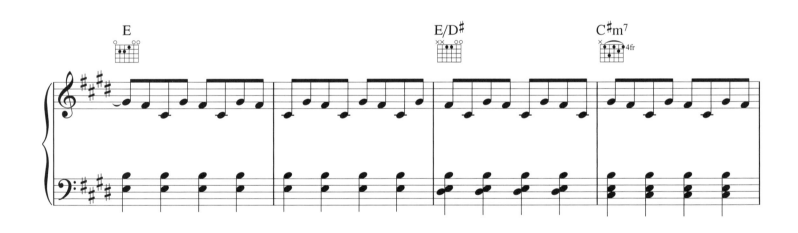

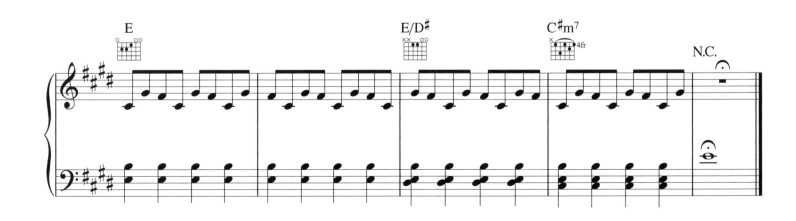

The Lightning Strike

(iii) Daybreak

Words & Music by Paul Wilson, Gary Lightbody,
Jonathan Quinn, Nathan Connolly & Tom Simpson

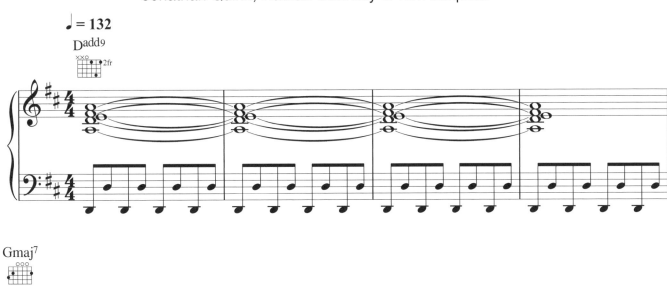

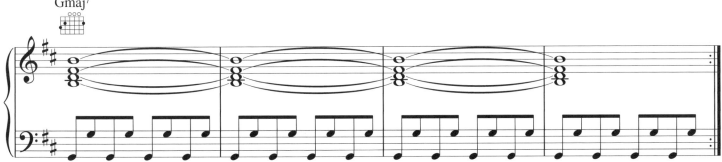

68

too _____ large   to   the   find _____
sky _____ and   the   cold _____

your _____ soul   in. _____   Some-thing was
mag _____ net   Earth. _____

Dsus²

bound _____ to   go _____ right   some - time   to - day.
mid - dle   of   the   flood   I   felt _____ my   worth. _____ When you

D   Gmaj⁷

All   these   bro-ken   piec - es   fit   to-geth - er   to   make _____
held   on-to   me   like   I   was _____ your   lit - tle   life   raft.   Please _____

_____ a   per - fect   pic - ture   of   us._____   It got
_____ know   that   you were   mine as   well.   Drops of

Dsus²

cold and then   dark_ so sud - den - ly and rained.   It rained   so   hard   the two
wa - ter hit the ground like God's_ own_ tears_   and spread out in - to shapes   like sal -

D   **Gmaj⁷**

of   us   were   the on - ly thing   that we_____ could
-ad   bowls_   and ba - sins   and buck - ets   for

1, 3.   **2, 4.**

D.S. al Coda

see for   miles_   and miles._____   And in the   _____   2. As
bail - ing   out_   the flood._____